FRIED CHICKEN AND CHORIZO

*The Unconditional Love and
Support of My Abuelita*

by

James Bass

Published by Clarice Jefferies Publishing

Contact info: cjpublishing@yahoo.com

For permissions contact: cjpublishing@yahoo.com

Printed in the United States of America on responsibly sourced paper

TABLE OF CONTENTS

1974–1980

*P*inche puta[1]! Pinche mayate[2]! Pinche puta amante de los mayates[3]! These are the insults that the Mexicans would shout at my grandmother and me as we walked down our neighborhood street to Hanoians Grocery Market. Some of these people were bold enough to spit on us as we walked. I remember my Abuelita[4] would pick me up and try to cover my face with her shirt to keep their spit from landing on my face. The ironic thing about this situation is… most of these Mexican men and women were darker than I was.

Those are some of the earliest memories of prejudice I can recall while living with my Abuelita. My Abuelita's name was Esperanza, which translates into "Hope" in English. This woman loved me unconditionally despite my dark skin color. She never treated me differently because of my appearance, and was never ashamed to be seen with me in public. Due to my dark skin color, she gave me extra love and understanding because she knew that my growing up would be a difficult journey.

My Abuelita never really shared much with me regarding her childhood, but from what little she did share, I understood

---

1   Fucking whore.
2   Fucking nigger.
3   Fucking nigger lover.
4   Granny.

it was rough and challenging. Like so many other Mexican men and women, my Abuelita left her home in Guadalajara, Mexico, and came to the United States in search of a better life leaving behind my mother's father, who refused to relocate to the US with her.

My mother was born years later here in Fresno, California, and I would be born decades later... And that's when the beautiful journey of my Abuelita and me began.

For those of you that have not yet had an opportunity to read my first book, *In Love with My 5 Wives*, it gives you an arduous, brutal journey into my difficult beginnings on this earth as a mixed-race, African American and Mexican American young man. *In Love with My 5 Wives* describes in graphic detail what my life was like growing up with my abusive mother and two abusive stepfathers. It also explains my difficult transition from being a violent and angry child, teenager and young man into a loving person and a loving husband.

In this book, *Fried Chicken and Chorizo*, I will share stories and thoughts, in no particular order, of what my life was like growing up with my Abuelita and the unconditional love and support I received from her.

EARLY 1980's

There was something magical about waking up early Saturday mornings at my Abuelita's house. It was so magical that Saturday morning cartoons were not even on my radar. I could always count on waking up to the sound of Radio Bilingüe (her favorite radio station) and the smell of *chorizo con huevos*[5], along with *papitas*[6] and homemade flour tortillas.

I would lay awake in bed and listen to the birds chirping, our dogs barking, and my grandmother singing as she cooked. Then she would call out, "*¡¡Jaimiiito!! ¡Ven a comerrrr!*"[7] I would jump out of bed and run into the kitchen, sliding along the old linoleum floor in my *calcetines*[8] and Superman *chonchos*[9]. My Abuelita would laugh and tell me to go and get dressed. So, I would return to my room, get dressed, and run back into the kitchen. I would give my Abuelita a big hug and sit down to eat.

From the time I was born until I was around four years old, I lived with my Abuelita. Then, when my mother married my younger brother's father, Sid, they got an apartment together, and I lived with them, but I still spent significant amounts of time with my Abuelita.

When I was a child, it was difficult for my mother to deal with the discriminatory treatment she would receive from Mexican people, white people, and society. It was embarrassing for her to be seen carrying this "Black kid". So, my mother would dump me at my Abuelita's house whenever she had the chance. And, of course, I was excellent with that.

---

5   Chorizo and fried eggs.
6   Fried potatoes.
7   "James, come and eat!"
8   Socks.
9   Underwear.

PRETTY BOY

Like most Mexican grandmothers, my Abuelita was heavily involved with the Catholic Church. My Abuelita was a proud member of the Virgen De Guadalupe club and participated in every church function imaginable… and she dragged me to almost every single one. If the church had Bingo night… I was there. If the church was serving breakfast or dinner as a fundraiser… I was there. If the church was having a community clean-up… I was there. For Palm Sunday, I was there. For Christmas church *posadas*[10], I was there. I participated in these church functions not by choice but out of necessity. My Abuelita was trying to keep me out of trouble. Little did I realize she was saving my life.

My home life with my mother and stepfather was extremely violent and abusive, and as a result, I developed an awful, vicious temper. I developed a tendency to fight for any and every reason. My Abuelita would take me to church as a way of not only spending quality time with me but also as a way of keeping me in a "safe" place. She did not realize that by taking me to church, she was endangering the safety of other kids, primarily Pretty Boy.

10　Literally, "the Inns" in English. A Christmas religious tradition that commemorates Maria and Joseph's journey from Nazareth to Bethlehem.

Pretty Boy was a kid that was in my catechism class. I went to catechism class (Sunday school) every Sunday and Wednesday, and as usual, I was the only Black kid there. I was teased a lot by the other kids. I was constantly being called a *mayate*[11]. A lot of kids made it a point not to sit next to me during prayer or while eating lunch or dinner, and a vast majority of the kids would flat-out ignore me. Sometimes I could shake off this treatment, but it often infuriated me.

I dealt with this treatment every Wednesday and Sunday for years, and as time went on, I began to notice that many of these kids would gravitate around Pretty Boy. They would hang out with him before class, hang out with him in between classes, and hang out with him after class. The kids would be talking and laughing with him, and after leaving Pretty Boy, that's when a lot of this discriminatory treatment towards me would begin. I would catch Pretty Boy staring at me from across the hallway or the cafeteria with a sarcastic grin. I recognized the look he was giving me. It was a look I had become very familiar with, and it was a look I had received from my people many times before; the look conveyed to me, "You don't belong here. This is my world."

Pretty Boy was a good-looking kid. His parents took excellent care of him, and he seemed to come from money. He was always dressed in the latest fashion from head to toe and never wore the same clothes or shoes twice. His hair was

---

11   Nigger.

picture-perfect, neatly combed, without a single strand of hair out of place. The girls couldn't resist him, and the boys wanted to be like him. He was a modern-day Ricky Martin, a pretty boy… And I wanted revenge for how he orchestrated my treatment. It was Sunday evening, and I decided I would get revenge on Wednesday.

On Wednesday, we all lined up in the hallway and waited for our teacher to take a head count and escort us into our classroom. I was leaning against the wall with my hands in my pockets as I watched Pretty Boy float past me with a trail of girls following him. Our eyes locked on each other as he walked by, and just before he was out of sight, he curled up the corner of his lips, giving me that sarcastic, evil smile of his… and that was all the invitation I needed.

We marched into the classroom in a single-file line and stood over the area where we were going to sit. I stood at the rear of the room with my back against the wall, and I watched the remainder of the kids march through the door and form single-file lines in front of me. I saw Pretty Boy walk in, and my blood began to boil. My rage meter began to fill with pure malice and revenge. The pages of my mental Rolodex began to spin out of control, searching for the appropriate level of suffering I could inflict on Pretty Boy. The other kids around me were yelling, laughing, and having a good time, but I could not hear anything. I lost my ability to see anything out of my peripheral vision, and all empathy immediately left my body. It felt like I had been instantly transported into a dark tunnel, and instead of seeing the light at the end, all I could see was Pretty Boy. I walked to the teacher's desk and grabbed a freshly sharpened number 2 pencil. I slithered my way through the kids in front of me as they playfully laughed and joked, pushing and shoving each other side to side.

I quickly walked up behind him, passing him on his left, and I took the pencil and buried it deep into the lower right side of his back. I could feel the pencil snap as I rushed forward, passing him. Pretty Boy let out a scream as he spun around, falling to the floor, clutching the right side of his body. I dropped the other half of the pencil in the trashcan as I walked out of the classroom. All the focus and attention immediately fell onto Pretty Boy as everyone huddled around him, trying to figure out what had happened.

Somebody called, and they had to take him to the hospital. The teachers and staff questioned me, but since no one had witnessed what happened, there was not much they could do about it. They called my Abuelita to the classroom and told her what had happened. They told her they felt like I was the one who stabbed Pretty Boy. I was sitting in the chair with my head down, staring at the carpet. My Abuelita walked over to me and put her hand under my chin. She raised my head so that I could see her. I looked at her with a look of defeat on my face as my eyes began to water. "*Ay, mijo*[12]," she said with empathy

12 "Oh, son…"

as she hugged me tightly. My Abuelita knew I had reached my breaking point behind all the racial bullshit I had been dealing with up to that point.

I was removed from that classroom and transferred to another room. Pretty Boy never returned to Catechism class.

My "People" Are Turning On Me

In the late 1980s, the rap song "Colors" came out. It was a song performed by Ice T and the title song on the movie *Colors'* soundtrack. The movie was a powerful depiction of gang life in South Central Los Angeles, and it also depicted the rivalry between two gangs, the Bloods and the Crips.

In the movie, and generally speaking, the Bloods and Crips were primarily portrayed as two Black gangs, and the rivalry between the two gangs was extremely bloody. However, when gang culture began to gain traction and flourish here in Fresno, California, the Bloods were primarily a Mexican gang, and the Crips were mainly a Black gang. When the movie was released, everything took a turn for the worse for me.

I was attending Middle School when the movie *Colors* was released just before summer vacation. I attended the school with many kids from my neighborhood and had known many of my classmates since elementary school. Many of these guys were like me, troubled youths that were always getting into fights, ditching class, and just all around up to no good. We got along incredibly, but that changed after *Colors* came out.

After the summer break, when we all returned to school, many of my Mexican-American "friends" were now Bloods, and they had a problem with all Black guys... and that included me.

I remember the first day of school; I saw one of my "friends" walking down the hall. I walked up behind him, tapped him on his shoulder and said, "Hey, man, what's up?" I was going to ask him what he did over summer vacation, but instead of greeting me, he turned around, saw it was me and shoved me hard while shouting, "Fuck you, cuzz, this is blood over here!"

At first, I couldn't comprehend what was taking place. I had not watched the movie *Colors*, but I had watched the music video. I noticed my former friend was wearing a red rag hanging out of his front pocket. At this time, another "Blood" shoved me from behind and shouted, "What's up, cuzz?" Everything slowed down as I spun around to address the guy behind me. As I turned my head, my peripheral vision locked onto him: he was standing in the traditional 1980s Chicano pre-fight stance with one foot forward and both arms in the air.

As I spun around, I balled up my right hand into the tightest fist possible and cracked him right on the side of his jaw, just below his ear. The crowd of peers around us shouted "Oooooh!" as he fell onto the concrete floor like a bag of cement; he lay unconscious. I spun around again, and my former friend yelled out, "Mother-fuckin nigger!" as he rushed toward me. He threw a wild punch that missed my face. I leaned to my right as I caught him with a left cross that broke his nose and then a right punch that landed square on his mouth.

Two counselors serving as hallway monitors rushed us and broke up the fight. The three of us were taken to the office, and somebody called our parents. The two boys' parents showed up first. Both of their parents were upset as they walked in and saw the condition of their sons. The first boy I hit, the one that shoved me from behind, was bleeding from his left ear, and the side of his forehead was swollen from hitting the concrete after being knocked unconscious. My former friend had a broken nose and a busted upper lip.

Their parents began to argue with one of the Spanish-speaking counselors demanding the police be called; they wanted to press charges. Their parents were calling me all kinds of *"pinche mayate*[13]*"* and *"sucio, greñuudo negrito*[14]*"*, not realizing that I could understand everything they were saying.

Then, my Abuelita rushed into the office and saw me sitting in the chair. I stood up as my Abuelita called out, *"Jaime, mijo, ¿qué pasó?*[15]*"* My Abuelita rushed over, hugged me, and began to look me over, checking my face and hands. Once she realized I was okay, she turned and looked at the two boys sitting there with their parents. The look on all of their faces was priceless! They were speechless as they stared at my grandmother and me. My grandmother cussed out their parents in Spanish, telling them they should be ashamed of themselves for their sons' behavior.

---

13 "Fucking nigger."
14 "Dirty, grimy little Black guy."
15 "James, son, what happened?"

The father of the boy that was knocked unconscious asked my grandmother, *"¿Este mayate es tu hijo?*[16]*"* My grandmother stuck her chest out with pride, raised her chin, and shouted back at him, *"Sí, cabrón, es mi hijo. ¿Y cómo que mayate? ¿Te has mirando en un espejo? ¡¡¡Tu culo es más negro que el suyo!!!*[17]*"* I chuckled as my Abuelita put her arm around me. He stood there speechless.

The silence lasted for a couple of seconds until one of the Spanish-speaking counselors explained to both of the boys parents that some teachers and hallway monitors instructed many other kids to report to the office. Most of those kids confirmed the two boys started the fight and tried to jump me. My grandmother looked at them and shook her head in disgust. One of the mothers apologized to my Abuelita, but my Abuelita didn't answer. Instead, my Abuelita put her hand on my shoulder and told me, *"Mijo,* let's go home."

---

16   "This nigger is your son?"
17   "Yes, fucker, this is my son. And what do you mean, 'nigger?' Have you looked in a mirror? Your ass is blacker than his!"

BACK TO
SCHOOL NIGHT

We would have a back-to-school night several times during the school year. I'm not sure if the schools still do that now… but I hated it! For those who don't know what back-to-school night is, it is a chance for your parents to come to the school for a meeting with all your teachers. Your parents would get a printout or list of all 6 or 7 classes; on that printout was your classroom number and teacher's name. The back-to-school night usually began around 4:30 pm and ended around 8 pm. Your parents would spend time walking from classroom to classroom, meeting all of your teachers, and discussing your grades along with how well you were… or were not progressing in the class.

I had this one teacher. I will call him Mr. M.

Mr. M was a first-class dickhead, a real prick. He took pleasure in looking down his nose at us over the rim of his glasses with disdain. He enjoyed humiliating us kids during class if we didn't understand what he was explaining. He was not born in the United States; he was originally from another country, I believe from France, and he thought he was better than anyone or anything walking the halls of our school. I disliked him. His hostile demeanor reminded me of Rock (my stepfather, chapter 2 of *In Love with My 5 Wives*).

On the day of back-to-school night, Mr. M periodically took the time to walk back and forth in front of my desk, expressing how much joy he would have telling my parents what an "incompetent nuisance" I was. He was going to spare no detail telling my parents how much he did not enjoy having me in his class. I got upset and told him to go shove a French baguette up his ass, and all of the kids died of laughter. He just chuckled as he looked down at me sitting at my desk and said, "Ahhhh, yes, I'm really going to enjoy this evening."

4:30 pm rolled around, and my little brother and mother got into the car and headed for my school. When we arrived and pulled into the parking lot, my Abuelita was already waiting for us. My little brother and I got out of the car and ran to her. We gave her a bunch of hugs and kisses and said, "*Hola, Abuelita*[18]." My mother watched with envy as she casually said, "Hey, mom." Then our mother yelled, "Hurry up and get over here; let's get this over with!"

We walked around to my first few classrooms, and my mother met with my teachers. They discussed my grades, classroom behavior, and overall attitude. My teachers also discussed with her the areas in which I needed to improve. Although my grades were not so excellent, and my attitude and behavior could have been better, my first few teachers gave me positive reviews.

18 "Hi, grandma."

Now... Mr. M. As we walked down the hall towards Mr. M's classroom, all I could think about was, *"Boy, am I going to get my ass demolished when I get home."* My mind flashed this image of Mr. M's face displaying a devilish grin, similar to *The Grinch*, as he gave my mother the rundown regarding my horrible grades and attitude.

We arrived at Mr. M's classroom and walked in. It was packed. There were a lot of parents in his class and a bunch of little kids running around all over the place. I spotted Mr. M at the back of the classroom talking to one of my friend's parents. I could see the terrified look on my friend's face as Mr. M gave his parents the rundown. I know my classmate was thinking the same thing I was, that he would get his ass beat when he got home.

We made our way up to the front of the classroom, where Mr. M posted everyone's failing grades on the wall. As we walked towards the front, my little brother began to wail as he jumped up and down, shouting he needed to use the bathroom. My mother told him to hold it, but he yelled, "I can't, mom. I have to go number 2!" He was dancing around with his hands covering his butt. My mother grabbed my little brother's hand and yelled, "C'mon," as she stormed out of the classroom.

Mr. M heard my mother's voice as she yelled out, and he noticed me standing at the front. I turned around to look for my grandmother, but she was at the back of the classroom, looking at the different pictures and assignments on the wall. Mr. M told the parents he was talking to, "Would you please excuse me?" And he walked away from them and eagerly approached me. "And where are your parents, young man?" he asked. He had this smirk on his face as he unfolded his arms and began rubbing his hands together like he was concocting the most devilish, horrible review to deliver to my mother.

"She's over there," I pointed to my Abuelita at the rear of the classroom. Mr. M looked around for a few seconds, scanning the back of the classroom, then he looked back at me and asked, "Ummm, where *exactly* is your mother." I pointed directly at my Abuelita as she made her way to the other side of the classroom. I said, "That's my mom right there."

Mr. M looked at my grandmother, looked back at me, looked at my grandmother once again, and chuckled. "Is that how you want to play this game? You certainly don't disappoint me, young man… Shall we?" He extended his hand outward, gesturing for me to walk towards the old woman I had just pointed out. As we approached my Abuelita, I began to say "*Abuel…*" but Mr. M eagerly interrupted me and said, "Excuse me, madam. I apologize, but this troubled young man has decided to involve you in his terrible prank. You see, madam, this young man has told me that you… are his mother." Mr. M began to chuckle.

30

My grandmother looked at Mr. M, looked at me, then looked at Mr. M again and said, "*Sí*, this is my son." Mr. M's smirk slowly turned to a stern look as he put his hand on my shoulder. He removed his glasses from his face and used them to direct his words like he was conducting an orchestra. "No, ma'am," he began. "There is no need for you to cover for this young man. You see, this is one of my 'troubled' students, and I only partook in his story of calling you his mother to show him that lying was not going to get him out of trouble."

My grandmother looked down at me and then looked back at Mr. M and repeated herself, but this time she said in Spanish, "*Sí, señor, es mi hijo*[19]." Mr. M's eyes got wide as he chuckled. "Ohhhh, ha ha ha. I do beg your apologies, madam. You are a Mexican. Of course, you don't understand our conversation. Oh, I do beg your pardon."

"*¡¿Este cabrón*[20]*?!*" My grandmother said. I chuckled as I told Mr. M, "No, she understands you; she told you yes, I am her son." Mr. M stood straight, looked over at me, and asked, "James, who is this woman? Where did you find her? And where, young man, are your parents?"

My grandmother shook her head. She asked me, "*¿Es este el pendejo racista del que has estando hablando*[21]*?*" "*Sí, Abuelita. Este es él*[22]." Mr. M stood there astonished as he watched my

---

19   "Yes, sir, this is my son."
20   "This fucker?!"
21   "Is this the racist asshole you have been talking about?"
22   "Yes, grandma, this is him."

grandmother and I talk to one another. My grandmother shook her head. She opened up her purse and pulled out a little wallet-sized photo album. She turned to Mr. M and began to flip through the album, showing him several baby pictures of her and me. *"Mira,"* she said, *"él es mi hijo*[23]*."*

Mr. M slowly took the photo album from my grandmother. His mouth was open in disbelief as he flipped through the pictures one by one, studying them carefully. "But... but... I don't understand," he said. "This cannot be. It just does not add up." My Abuelita snatched the photo album from his hands. *"Humph! ¿Y por qué no*[24]*?"* Mr. M turned to me, waiting for the translation with a look of confusion plastered across his face. It was the first time I had seen him speechless. I told him, "She asked you, and why not?"

Mr. M paused for a second, looked at my grandmother, and stammered, "Wwwell... well, because... he is Black... and you are a Mexican. It just does not make sense. I mean, look at the color of his skin; he is so dark. He is a Black boy... There is no way possible and, no way biologically, that he has an ounce of Mexican blood in his body."

My Abuelita lost all composure. She spit at his feet and shouted, *"¡Hijo de puta! ¡Me cago en tu tumba! ¡No puedo creer que te empleen para enseñar a los niños, bastardo racista!*[25]*"*

---

23 "Look," she said, "he is my son."
24 "Hmph! and why not?"
25 "Son of a bitch! I'll shit on your grave! I can't believe they employ you as a teacher for children, you racist bastard!"

Mr. M got really quiet. The other parents in the classroom stopped what they were doing and looked over at us. Mr. M took the tip of his shoe and tried to wipe away my Abuelita's spit from the floor. He looked at her sternly, eye to eye, as he asked me, "Well, young man, if you would be so kind as to translate."

I said, "Ummm, yeah," as I scratched my head. "She said you are a sorry ass son of a bitch, and she is going to shit on your grave." The classroom came to a screeching halt as the other parents and children looked at us in disbelief. Mr. M turned his head to face me with wide-open eyes. "And she called you a racist bastard and said she can't believe you have a job teaching children."

"*¡Hijo, vámonos*[26]*!*" My grandmother reached for my hand. "Bye," I told Mr. M as I waved, leaving the classroom. As we were walking out, my mother walked in with my little brother. "*¡Adónde vas*[27]*?*" My mother asked. "*¡A mi casa!*" my Abuelita shouted, "*¡Y me llevo a Jaime conmigo*[28]*!*"

---

26 "Son, let's go!"
27 "Where are you going?"
28 "Home! And I'm taking James with me!"

Abuelita "Breaks Bread" With the Crips

I went to Sequoia for the 9th grade. It is a 7th and 8th-grade middle school today, but back in the 1980s, it was a freshman school only. It was wild back then; the school was full of troubled teens that were one step away from continuation school or juvenile hall. The Bloods' and Crips' gang activity and culture were still in full swing, and that culture was still wreaking havoc in our neighborhoods and my life.

The school was located right in the middle of our neighborhood. My Abuelita's house was situated on Dwight Way. The front entrance to the school is located on Hamilton Street, two blocks north of Dwight Way. The back entrance to the school is located on Woodward Ave, one block north of Dwight Way. The school's back entrance was where it all went down. All of the fights, stabbings, and drive-by shootings.

Unfortunately, I had one of two ways to walk to my Abuelita's house after school. I could walk out of the rear gate on Woodward Ave and head east towards Cedar Ave, then walk south on Cedar Ave. to Dwight Way, then turn west, down Dwight Way to my Abuelita's; that would be the "safest" choice. Or I could take a shortcut and walk down 9th Street, nicknamed Blood Alley because that short street strip had a lot of blood gang activity. I didn't feel like fighting for my life on this particular day, so I chose to walk down Cedar Ave.

Cedar Ave. is a major, four-lane street in Fresno, Ca. Cedar Ave. has two lanes going north and two lanes going south. As I walked south on Cedar and turned right onto Dwight Way, a group of three Bloods stood across the street in front of an apartment complex. They were drinking beer and smoking "Caviar" or "Cavi's," a popular street name in the 1980s given to a marijuana joint laced with cocaine. As I turned the corner, I caught one of the guy's attention. He yelled out, "What's up, cuzz! This Blood over here!" I just ignored him and began to walk a little bit more quickly. I heard a different voice yell out, "¿Estás perdido, mayate[29]?" I didn't pay them any attention, and I continued to walk. Then, I heard the sound of breaking glass. I glanced over my shoulder and saw all three of them running towards me. One of the guys had a broken beer bottle in his hand. I dropped my backpack and began to run.

I ran as quickly as I could down the street towards my Abueilta's, but I could hear the laughter and footsteps getting closer and closer. A beer bottle was thrown, flew by me, and shattered on the street just a few feet before me. I could hear the footsteps directly behind me, and I was running out of breath. I stopped and spun around, I had no choice but to fight with these three assholes, but as I turned around, the odds had drastically changed.

---

29 "Are you lost, nigger?"

As I turned to face my attackers, who were about 15 feet away, behind them... were four Crips.

As I stopped and planted my feet, the guy closest to me took a wild swing using his forward momentum. I dodged his haymaker as he flew by me, and as soon as he stopped to turn around, I hit him with a solid right cross that sent him backward on the street. I turned around to see where the other two guys were, and they were getting their asses handed to them by their gang rivals. The Crips were mopping the street with these guys, beating the dog shit out of them. I turned around to see where the first guy was; he was having difficulty getting to his feet. I stood a few feet in front of him, waiting for him to square up with me, but he raised one hand as if to say, "Don't," as he used his other hand to keep from falling back onto the street. He was extremely dizzy and was bleeding pretty badly from his mouth. I could see that his jaw was broken as he held his chin with his other hand. He was able to make it to his feet and run past me. I looked at the Crips, and they had finished trying to stomp holes into the other two guys as they made it to their feet and began running away.

I watched all three Bloods run away as the Crips yelled out, "That's what's up, cuzz!" as they made their signature letter C with their hands and raised them triumphantly in the air. As they approached me, one of them asked, "Damn, cuzz, the fuck you doing in this hood?"

"I was walking to my grandmother's house," I replied, trying to catch my breath. One of the other Crips asked, "Damn, cuzz, yo grand-momma stay in this hood?" I said, "Yes, my house is right there." I pointed to my abuelitas house, about four houses away. The other two Crips shook their heads and said, "Damn." The first Crip that asked me what I was doing in the neighborhood said, "Alright then, cuzz, we will walk with you just in case them slobs[30] come back." I said, "Thanks," and asked them, "Where did you guys come from?" One of the guys replied, "We was on bus 38. We saw you running down the street being chased by them slobs. I pulled the string and yelled, 'Stop this mutha-fuckin bus!' We all ran off the bus and started chasing them niggas that was chasing you."

I was very grateful to these four guys, so I said, "Thank you." "We got yo back, my nigga!" he replied as we shook hands.

The five of us began to walk down the street. The Crips began to laugh and pump each other up as they replayed the fight that had just taken place step by step. I increasingly got nervous as we got closer and closer to my Abuelita's house. I hoped she was not outside, but as we got closer to my home, I could see my Abuelita sitting on the porch, crocheting and blasting Vicente Fernandez from the radio.

I didn't say anything. I guess a part of me hoped they wouldn't notice the "little old Mexican lady" sitting outside,

30 A derogatory term used by Crips towards the Bloods.

but as I approached the gate, one of the Crips said, "A yo! What the fuck, cuzz?" I quickly reached for the gate, opened it, and stepped inside the yard, saying, "Well, thanks a lot, guys." The shock and confusion on their faces were disturbing, but I was all too familiar with that reaction from people.

"I thought you said you were walking to yo grand-momma's house, cuzz," one of the Crips shouted. Before I could answer, my Abuelita stood up from the porch and shouted, "Hi, *mijo, ¿quiénes son tus amigos[31]?*" "*Estos son mis amigos de la escuela[32].*" I replied. The Crips just looked at each other in disbelief. My grandmother walked down a few steps from the porch and waved to them, "*Buenas tardes, bienvenidos a nuestra casa.[33]*"

The Crips, with their mouths still open, looked at me. I told them, "My grandmother said hello and welcome to our home." One of the Crips waved back to my Abuelita as the other three gave him a look as if to say, what the hell are you doing? My grandmother walked down a few more steps and said, "*Si ustedes tienen hambre, entren a comer.[34]*" The Crips looked at me again for translation, so I told them, "My grandmother said if you guys are hungry, come inside so you can eat."

My grandmother turned and walked back up the steps and went inside the house. I looked at all four of them and opened the gate. I said, "C'mon, it's cool." I walked inside the yard and

31 "Hi, son, who are your friends?"
32 "These are my friends from school."
33 "Good afternoon, welcome to our home."
34 "If you are hungry, come on in and eat."

walked down the dirt path. I glanced over my shoulder and saw the four guys reluctantly enter the yard. They didn't say anything, they just followed behind me, so I turned around and made my way up the steps and to the front door. The front door was open, and you could smell all the food from the kitchen. One of the guys said, "Damn, cuzz, it smells good." The other guy said, "Man, I love Mexican food." I just smiled as I opened the security gate. I held the door open as they walked through. Their eyes looked around at the walls with all my baby pictures. Then they saw a picture of my mother and me and more photos of my Abuelita and me.

One of the guys asked, "Ah, cuzz... Are you Mexican?" the others looked at me with curiosity. I said, "I'm mixed. My dad is Black, and my mother is Mexican." They chuckled and said, "Damn!" I could tell the scene was beginning to make sense to them. I started walking throughout the house, showing them all the pictures on the walls and explaining who each person was.

"This is my mother," I pointed to one picture. "This is my little brother and me, my aunts and uncles, and these people over here are my cousins." One of the Crips interrupted and asked, "Where is yo daddy, cuzz?" "I don't know," I replied. "I don't know my dad. He never comes around. I've never met him." One of the other Crips asked, "You never met yo daddy? You only been raised by yo Mexican momma?" "Yes, and my grandmother," I replied.

One of the other Crips said, "Yeah, my daddy don't come around either." "Neither does mine" the other replied. The third Crip said, "My daddy's locked up," and the fourth said, "My daddy was killed in a drive-by in LA; that's how we ended up in Fresno. My momma moved us here to get away from that shit, but it's the same down here."

As we talked, my grandmother had been bringing big pots and pans of food from the kitchen and placing them on the dining room table. My grandmother made chicken and mole, Spanish rice, flour tortillas, and chicharrones. She said in her best broken English, "Okay, the food is ready." We turned around, and the guys just stared at all of the food. One of them said, "Damn, nigga, this smells good!" The other guy standing close gave him a quick elbow to the ribs as if to say, "Show some respect." The guy corrected his behavior by saying, "I'm sorry, ma'am; I mean, this food looks really good." My grandmother walked up to him, put one hand on his shoulder, and said, "*Mijo*, my house is your house."

My grandmother turned and looked at all of them and said, "*Gracias por ayudar a mi hijo*[35]."

We all sat down at the table to eat. My grandmother, her dark, half-breed grandson, and four members of the Crip family.

---

35 "Thank you for helping my son."

Years later, I asked my grandmother if she remembered that day. She said, "*Sí, mijo. Sabía que estabas teniendo problemas con los chicos de la esquina. Oré por tu protección en tu camino a casa. Esos cuatro tipos eran tus ángeles guardianes*[36]."

---

36 "Yes, son. I knew you were having problems with those guys at the corner, and I prayed for your protection on your way home. Those four guys were your guardian angels."

My "First" Haircut

When I was younger, I struggled to feel comfortable in my skin. I had a lot of mixed feelings and emotions regarding being a mixed race… Black and Mexican, Black child. Although mixed, I looked like your "typical" Black kid. I was skinny, and dark-skinned with an afro, but I was being raised in Mexican cultures, like your "typical" Mexican kid. This was creating a conflict within me that I couldn't quite understand. Still, my Abuelita could pick up on it, so she decided she would do her best to get me to "identify" and feel more comfortable in my black skin; she took me to get a Jeri Curl.

My Abuelita made an appointment with her hairdresser and took me to the beauty salon, and about 1 hr later, I came out with the tightest, wettest, shiniest head full of curls you could ever imagine, and my self-esteem shot to the moon. When I got home and looked in the mirror, I couldn't believe my eyes; for the first time, I felt "Black." I gave my Abuelita the biggest hug, ran into the living room, popped in my Michael Jackson VHS tape, and began to dance and practice his dance moves.

Later that year, for Halloween, my Abuelita purchased me a look-a-like Michael Jackson outfit remarkably similar to the one he wore when he debuted the Moonwalk during his Billie Jean performance in 1983. I dressed up as Michael Jackson and entered a Halloween contest, lip-syncing and performing a rendition of Bille Jean, and I won first place! My Abuelita was so proud.

All of the "Blackness" was too much for my stepfather Rock, so he decided to end all this "Black bullshit" by taking me down to the barbershop and having my head shaved. Yes, Rock, had the barber shave all of my hair off! Down to my scalp. The ironic thing about this situation was that Rock drove me to the West Side of Fresno to a Black barbershop to have this done. Tears ran down my cheeks as the barber reluctantly shaved off all of my hair, and just like that…my "Blackness" was stripped away from me.

The following week, when my Abuelita came to pick me up for church, I ran into her arms with tears. She couldn't believe what she was seeing. She pulled me away from her and stood me in front of her. I felt so embarrassed and ashamed; I could only stare at the floor. She ran the palm of her hand across my bald head. My Abuelitas face got red, and her eyes began to water as she asked me, *"Mijo, ¿qué le pasó a tu cabello? ¿Quién lo cortó?*[37]*"* I told her, *"Rock me llevó a la peluquería y le dijo al peluquero que me cortara todo el pelo*[38]*."*

---

37 "Son, what happened to your hair? Who cut it?"
38 "Rock took me to the barbershop and told the barber to cut off all my hair."

My Abuelita became furious and shouted for Rock to enter the dining room. Rock never came out of his bedroom; instead, my mother asked my Abuelita what was happening. My Abuelita and mother proceeded to get into a humongous argument behind Rock and my haircut. I remember my Abuelita demanding that Rock reimburse her for the cost of my Jeri curl. My mother stormed out of the dining room and walked to her bedroom. She returned a few seconds later with a wad of dollar bills and tossed the money onto the table. My Abuelita picked up the money, grabbed her purse, and told me, "Let's go!"

We walked out of my mother's house and down the driveway. As we walked to the car, my mother was cussing out my Abuelita from the front door. We got into the car, and as I buckled my seatbelt, I looked up, and my Abuelita stuck her left arm out of the window and proceeded to give my mother the middle finger. She backed up out of the driveway, and we left.

As we drove down the street, I told my Abuelita, "*No tengo ganas de ir a la Iglesia*[39]." My Abuelita didn't say anything. I looked over at her, and she was looking forward, staring out of the windshield, driving with tears running down her cheeks. My Abuelita drove around for about 30 minutes; I sat quietly in the passenger seat, staring out the window. My Abuelita needed time to think and calm down before we went to church.

---

39 "I don't feel like attending church."

It wasn't too long after that my Abuelita pulled into the K-Mart parking lot. She told me to get out, and we walked into the store. My Abuelita walked up and down all of the aisles in the store until she found what she was looking for. She stopped, pointed at the shelf, and asked me, "*Mijo… ¿cuál*[40]*?*"

I looked up at the shelf and found myself staring at different brands, makes, and models of hair clippers for men. I looked at her confused, and she looked back at me and said, "*Nadie será responsable de cómo te ves de nuevo. A patir de ahora, vas a aprender a cortarte el pelo*[41]."

A slow smile came across my face. I gave my Abuelita a big hug and then turned to the shelf and tried to identify the clippers that I saw the barber use to shave my head. There were so many different options it was hard to choose; plus, I wasn't paying attention to what type of clippers the barber was using as my head was being shaved. My Abuelita stood there patiently as I looked at the pictures on the different boxes. I finally spotted a set similar to the ones I noticed at the barbershop. I pointed to the box and said, "*Estos*[42]."

My Abuelita grabbed the box and proceeded to walk to the checkout line. When we got to the cashier, my Abuelita reached into her purse and pulled out the wad of dollar bills my mother threw onto the dining room table. She pulled

---

40 "Son… which one?"
41 "No one will ever be responsible for how you look again. From now on, you're going to learn how to cut your hair."
42 "These."

apart, unwrinkled each bill, and used that money to pay for the clippers. The cashier put the clippers into a bag and handed the bag to my Abuelita. My Abuelita took the bag and gave it to me. She didn't say anything; she just smiled.

We left K-Mart, but we didn't go to church; we went home instead. I got out of the car and went to my room when we got home. I sat on my bed, took the clippers out of the box, plugged them into the wall, and turned them on. I will always remember that initial click and the buzzing hum from those clippers. I walked into the bathroom and looked at my head in the mirror. I didn't have enough hair to cut, so I put the clippers back into the box and put the box in my dresser drawer.

The following month I gave myself my first haircut, and it came out terrible!! I nicked my ears, nicked the back of my neck, had patches of hair missing, and my hairline looked like a road map... Crooked as hell! But I didn't care, I was determined to learn how to cut my hair, and after about six or seven months, I got good at it.

My Abuelita purchased those clippers when I was in junior high. I'm now 48 years old. Except for going to a barbershop a handful of times... I've been cutting my hair ever since.

My Recollection
My Mother Storms
Out of the Church

Around my Junior year in high school, my Abuelita thought it would be good to have me complete my "Recollection." In the Catholic religion, concerning the spiritual world, it is a type of ceremony or program that requires an individual to focus their complete attention on the presence of God. Part of the process is the withdrawal of your body and mind from all external and worldly experiences to focus on God and his teachings. So, for this process to occur, I would spend a weekend at church.

My Abuelita dropped me off at church on Friday after school, and I would not be allowed to go home until Sunday evening. When I arrived at church along with the rest of the usual bunch of troubled youth, I was required to bring only a change of clothes and toiletries. Food and everything else would be provided. We were not allowed to wear a watch or bring anything else. This was, of course, before the technological age we live in today, so cell phones, YouTube, Snap Chat, Instagram, Facebook, tablets, MP3s, and the internet did not exist.

During Friday evening, we studied the Bible teachings and the word of God, and we were required to reflect on our lives and how we conducted ourselves as young adults. Saturday, we did the same thing. Saturday evening, we were told to take everything we learned, think about everything that we were grateful for, and write our thoughts down on paper as a letter. We were informed that on Sunday morning we would be called up to the front of the church one at a time and read these letters out loud in front of our parents and the congregation. We all looked at each other in disbelief; we had no idea that our parents would be involved in this process.

When Sunday came, it was a challenging day for me. I was supposed to write this "love letter" to my parents, expressing how thankful and appreciative I was for having them in my life… but I was not. I hated my mother and my stepfather and was not grateful for very much of anything that had to do with either of them. I struggled with feeling like a hypocrite because what I felt went against every fiber in my body and everything I had been taught for those three days. So after a couple of hours of sitting alone feeling conflicted, I decided to write a letter of love and gratitude addressing my Abuelita.

Sunday morning finally came, and all of us teenagers filled the front four rows on the left and right sides of the church. We all turned around periodically, filled with nervous anticipation, as we watched all of the families fill the seats in the church. After about 30 minutes, the priest took his place at the Altar and began the ceremony. He opened with a prayer and then began to explain to all of the families the purpose of the Recollection ceremony that was about to take place. He explained to all of the parents and family members what we had studied during our time at the church and that each one of us would be called up to the alter, one at a time, and address our parents via "a letter of love and gratitude" that we had written. The priest instructed the parents that as we read our letter out loud, our parents were required to stand in honor of the recognition.

Now obviously, our parents knew about us spending three nights at the church because they had to sign our permission slips (my Abuelita signed mine). Still, they were unaware of the letters we would be reading to them because when the priest announced the reading of the letters, most of the parents gasped in disbelief, and most of the mothers and even some of the fathers began to shed some tears of joy.

I sat nervously as the priest called each one of us up one by one. There wasn't a dry eye in the church. I watched as some of the hardest, most brutal teenage boys and girls break down and cry as they read aloud to their parents everything they were grateful for and also apologized to their parents for all the trouble and heartache they had caused up to that point. Then the priest called my name...

As I stood up, all of the kids clapped. They knew a little about my story of abuse and neglect at the hands of my mother and stepfathers because late Saturday evening, during Recollection class, we all were required to share our life journey up to that point. As I walked to the front of the Altar, I kneeled before Christ and made the sign of the cross. I walked to the podium and took the letter from my back pocket. I unfolded the letter, took a deep breath, and looked out into the crowd. The pews were full, and it was standing room only. Easily there were probably around 500 people in the church.

I could see the familiar look of confusion and curiosity as some of the parents and family members looked around, trying to figure out who this Black kid was and where his parents were. The priest announced, "And now, will the parents of James Bass please stand." I looked out into the crowd, and to my shock and disbelief, my mother stood up. Yes, my actual biological mother was in church. I stood at the podium, frozen for a second, unable to catch my breath.

My mother hardly ever attended anything that had to do with the church. And she rarely attended anything church-related that had to do with me, and yet there she was, standing before me in church. I watched as the crowd of churchgoers leaned over towards one another in disbelief, whispering, "*¿Ella es su madre*[43]*?*"

The priest noted what was happening as the church buzzed with curiosity, so he stood up from his seat and walked towards me. "*Con permiso, discúlpame, hijo*[44]," he told me. I stepped to the side as he leaned towards the microphone, "And now, will the parents of James Bass please stand," he said once again.

---

43   "She is his mother?"
44   "Excuse me, son."

Everyone looked around the church. I was staring at my mother, and my mother was staring back at me. My mother was already standing, but she was standing there alone. The priest paused for a second, looked directly at the back of the church, and repeated a third time, "And now, will the parents of James Bass please stand." It was at this time I realized what was taking place.

Seated at the back of the church, by herself, in the last pew, was my Abuelita. She was not seated next to my mother, and my mother was sitting in the 6th or 7th pew. I was so shocked to see my mother in the church that I never asked myself, "Where is my Abuelita?"

The priest was staring at the back of the church, so all the churchgoers and family members turned around in their seats and began to look toward the back of the church. The priest said, "*Esperanza, levántate, por favor, y acércate*[45]."

As my Abuelita stood up, everyone who knew her (which was about half of the church) began clapping. Many other grandparents stood up and clapped as my Abuelita walked down the aisle. My Abuelita was overcome with emotion. She covered her mouth with one hand and began to cry as she stepped forward. I could no longer hold in my feelings, and I began to cry as I watched my Abuelita walk towards the front of the church. My Abuelita stopped at the row my mother was standing in. She

---

45   "Esperanza, stand up, please, and come forward."

gave me a wave and placed her hand over her heart. I waved back with tears of joy in my eyes as the church continued to give my Abuelita, my actual mother, her standing ovation.

The priest looked at me, nodded his head, and motioned for me to resume my place at the podium. He turned and walked back to his seat, and sat down. My Abuelita began to walk down the aisle to stand next to my mother. As the church began to simmer down, I could hear faint conversations as some of the families and newer church members asked the older church members what was happening.

The older members began to explain, "The first woman that stood up is James's biological mother. James is mixed with Black and Mexican, but his mother treats him like shit. Esperanza is his Abuelita, but she is the woman who truly loves James and has been raising him like her son."

My Abuelita made her way down the row and was now standing next to my mother. My Abuelita held my mother's hand, looked at me, and nodded, indicating that she was ready. I took a deep breath and began to read my letter. As I read my letter of gratitude, my Abuelita began to cry, and the more I read, my mother began to get angry. My mother realized that although the letter was supposed to be for our "parents," I briefly mentioned her and my stepfather; my letter was primarily addressed to my Abuelita. My letter was filled with gratitude, love, and appreciation regarding situations that only concerned my Abuelita and myself.

The other Mexican parents and grandparents began to stare at my mother, looking at her with disgust and disdain. My mother finally couldn't take the shame and embarrassment, so she let go of her mother's hand, grabbed her purse, and stormed out of the church. I paused from reading my letter as I, along with everyone else, watched her walk out. Once she left, I looked back at the priest, and he looked at me and nodded his head for me to continue. My Abuelita stood there alone as I finished reading my letter to her. When I finished, the church erupted with cheers, clapping, and giving my Abuelita another standing ovation.

FIGHTING WORDS: MI ABUELITA VS MI MAMÁ

One summer, we took a family trip to a very popular theme park in California. I went on this trip with my mother, stepfather, younger brother, and younger sister. We had been to this theme park many times before, but this particular occasion was special because my Abuelita was coming with us. I was a little older, around 12 or 13, and I had my own money to spend, about $150. I earned and saved this money from my summer job working with my *padrino*[46]. My *padrino* owned his own landscaping business, and I would work with him every summer during the weekends mowing lawns and raking leaves.

Once we arrived at the theme park, we did the usual thing: walk around and get on all of the rides that my stepfather, Rock, wanted to get on, which was cool with me. Although I was not too fond of Rock, I loved getting on all the roller coaster rides. After getting on the rides, we would walk around and get something to eat. My little brother, little sister, and I got the usual corn dogs and sodas. My Abuelita, mother, and Rock got hamburgers, French fries, and sodas, except Rock, who got his Coors beer.

We found an amphitheater area to sit and eat our food. The site was made of concrete and had stadium-type bench

---

46   Godfather.

seating, which led down to a stage at the center of the theatre. On this stage was something that looked like a cave. It was a small mound of dirt that looked like a miniature mountain and had a big hole in the center. It looked like, at any moment, something was going to pop out of it.

As we sat down to eat, many people began to come and sit at this amphitheater around us; some had food and drinks, and others just gathered around us, anxious to find a seat. I looked around, and the area was packed, with easily over 100 people, primarily adults and some children. Looking around at everyone, I began to get this panic type of feeling. My heart began to race and began to pound fiercely. I could feel my skin flush as I began to have a difficult time trying to catch my breath. I started frantically looking around, spinning my head from left to right, scanning the crowd around me. My Abuelita noticed my behavior and asked, "*Mijo, ¿qué pasó[47]?*" I looked at her with a face full of anxiety, and my Abuelita knew what I was feeling. She recognized the look on my face. She knew I realized I was the only Black kid amongst all of these white people.

She put down her food and stood up. She grabbed my hand and said, "*Vámonos[48].*" My mother asked her, "Where are you going? The show is about to start!" Before my grandmother could answer, some music began to play, and this little troll-looking puppet popped his head out of the cave. People began

---

47 "Son, what's wrong?"
48 "Let's go."

to clap and cheer as the troll puppet laughed and shook his head as he scanned the crowd. My grandmother and I sat back down because some people behind us complained they couldn't see. The show was starting, and little did I know I would be the main attraction.

This troll was a grumpy individual. He began to complain about his life as a troll and all the hardships it came with. Everyone was laughing at his jokes and applauding and having a good time. Then, the show turned odd; the troll began to focus on the audience. The troll started to pick on and talk about certain audience members, similar to a roast. We were seated towards the rear, in the center of this theatre. The troll started on the right and was making his way toward our direction. Up to this point, the troll had been making relatively harmless jokes about the white audience members. He had been cracking jokes about their hairstyles and choices of foods they were consuming, and he even cracked jokes about one guy's mustache and beard. My grandmother recognized what was taking place and realized he was making his way toward us. She quickly put her food down and stood up again, but this time she stated with urgency, "¡*Vamos, mijo, apúrate*[49]!" but it was too late; the troll spotted us and began to throw some of the most prejudice insults he could muster up.

I was wearing a pair of dark blue jeans, blue and white Puma tennis shoes, and a blue and grey Duke Blue devils basketball jersey. The troll looked at us and shouted, "Hey,

49 "Let's go, son, hurry!"

Duke, where are you going?" Everyone in the amphitheater turned and looked at us. I could feel my skin flush as the entire crowd stared at us. "Don't run now; the show is about to get good," the troll shouted. "Oh, but wait," he continued, "You people are good at running, good at running with a ball in your hands, good at running from the law, and good at running your mouth!" The whole crowd erupted with laughter... including my mother and Rock.

"I mean, look at him; he is even wearing a basketball jersey. That proves my point. Duke Blue devils? HA! Fat chance of you getting into that university; you better aim your sights a little lower than that, young man." I looked around and began to panic as most of the white people around us stared and laughed. My grandmother pulled me close to her side and hugged me as we stood there... The troll continued.

"D-U-K-E, do you even know what that spells?" he asked. "Can you even spell? Here, I will spell it out for you again, D-U-K-E. Do you even know what that stands for? It stands for Dumb Ugly Kids Everywhere, and you, young man, take the cake!"

My mother and Rock toppled over with laughter, along with the crowd of white people. The puppet added, "I mean, just look at him, big, dumb, and ugly; his shirt says it all!" My grandmother shouted, "¡Vete a la mierda, hombre títere[50]!" She tugged my arm as we made our way down the line of people,

---

50 "Fuck you, puppet man!"

walked up the few remaining steps, and exited the theatre. We got a few feet away, and I could no longer hold in my emotions; I broke down and began to cry out of pure rage, frustration, and embarrassment. My grandmother held me as I cried. I mumbled to her, "*Yo quiero matar a ese hombre*[51]." She rubbed my back and whispered, "*Lo sé, hijo, yo también*[52]."

A few minutes later, my mother and Rock came walking over toward us, and my mother began to yell at me, "What the fuck are you crying for? I swear, we can't take you anywhere. You always find a way to fuck up a good time." My Abuelita spun me behind her as she slapped my mother across her face, shouting. "*¿Qué diablos le pasa a él? No: ¿qué diablos te pasa a ti*[53]?" My mother held the left side of her cheek. She tried to lunge forward like she was going to shove my grandmother, but Rock grabbed her arm.

My abuelita shouted, "*Oh, ¿ahora estás enojada? ¿Ahora quires saltar y hacer algo? ¿Dónde estaba esa mujer mala cuando ese pinche gabacho estaba insultando a tu hijo*[54]?"

My grandmother and I walked off, leaving our "family" behind. We walked around the park for hours and talked to one another. At one point, my grandmother tried to find a way for us to get back to Fresno via a bus or some other form of

---

51 "I want to kill that man."
52 "I know, son, so do I."
53 "What the fuck is wrong with him? No: what the fuck is wrong with you?"
54 "Oh, now you are angry? Now you want to jump up and do something? Where was this bad ass woman when that fucking white man was insulting your son?"

transportation, but she was unsuccessful. As we walked around the park, some of the white people in the audience stepped up and apologized to my grandmother and me for what had happened. They stated how disgusted they were at how I was treated and they would complain to park management.

Many hours later, my Abuelita and I returned to the parking lot and met my mother and Rock at the van. My little brother and sister hugged me, and my little brother began to cry. It was a quiet ride home.

Abuelita's Words of Encouragement

As I got older, my Abuelita began to notice I was becoming increasingly angry and frustrated with the discriminatory treatment I was being bombarded with. She often tried to talk to me about not letting the horrible treatment get the best of me. She would often share stories with me regarding her struggles moving here from Guadalajara, Mexico, and how difficult it was for her to deal with the discriminatory treatment she received from white people during the '50s, '60s, and '70s. She would tell me although it was hard, she never lost sight of her ultimate goal of becoming a US citizen.

I remember the day I finally expressed my frustration and told her, "*Sí, Abuelita, pero mi situación es diferente*[55]."

"*¿Cómo es eso*[56]?" she asked.

"*No eres una mujer blanca. No estoy disculpando la forma en que los gabachos te han tratado, pero al fin y al cabo esa no es tu gente. Mi propia gente me trata mal porque no me parezco a ellos, y duele*[57]."

I began to cry as I put my head down on the kitchen table. My Abuelita walked over to me and placed her hands on my

---

55 "Yeah, grandma, but my situation is different."
56 "How so?"
57 "You are not a white woman. I'm not excusing the way white people have treated you, but at the end of the day, those are not your people. My own people are treating me wrong because I don't look like them, and it hurts."

shoulders. She leaned over and kissed me on the back of my head and said, *"Mijo, lo entiendo. Todo lo que estoy tratando de decir es que nunca dejé que el trato severo me impidiera ser una Mexicana orgullosa, y que eres afortunado de tener lo mejor de ambos mundos: todas nuestras fuerzas y ningua de nuestras debilidades. Nuestras culturas construyeron civilizaciones. Provienes de reyes[58]."*

I picked my head up off the table, turned around, and looked at my Abuelita. She smiled and said, *"La próxima vez que alguien te esté haciendo sentir mal por lo que eres, recuerda el amor que tengo por ti[59]."* I immediately began to feel better. I got up and gave my Abuelita a big hug and told her, *"Gracias, Abuelita, te amo[60]."*

---

58 "Son, I understand. All I'm trying to say is I never let the harsh treatment keep me from being a proud Mexican, and you are fortunate to have the best of both worlds: all of our strengths and none of our weaknesses. Our cultures built civilizations. You come from kings."
59 "The next time someone is making you feel bad because of who you are, remember the love I have for you."
60 "Thank you, grandma, I love you."

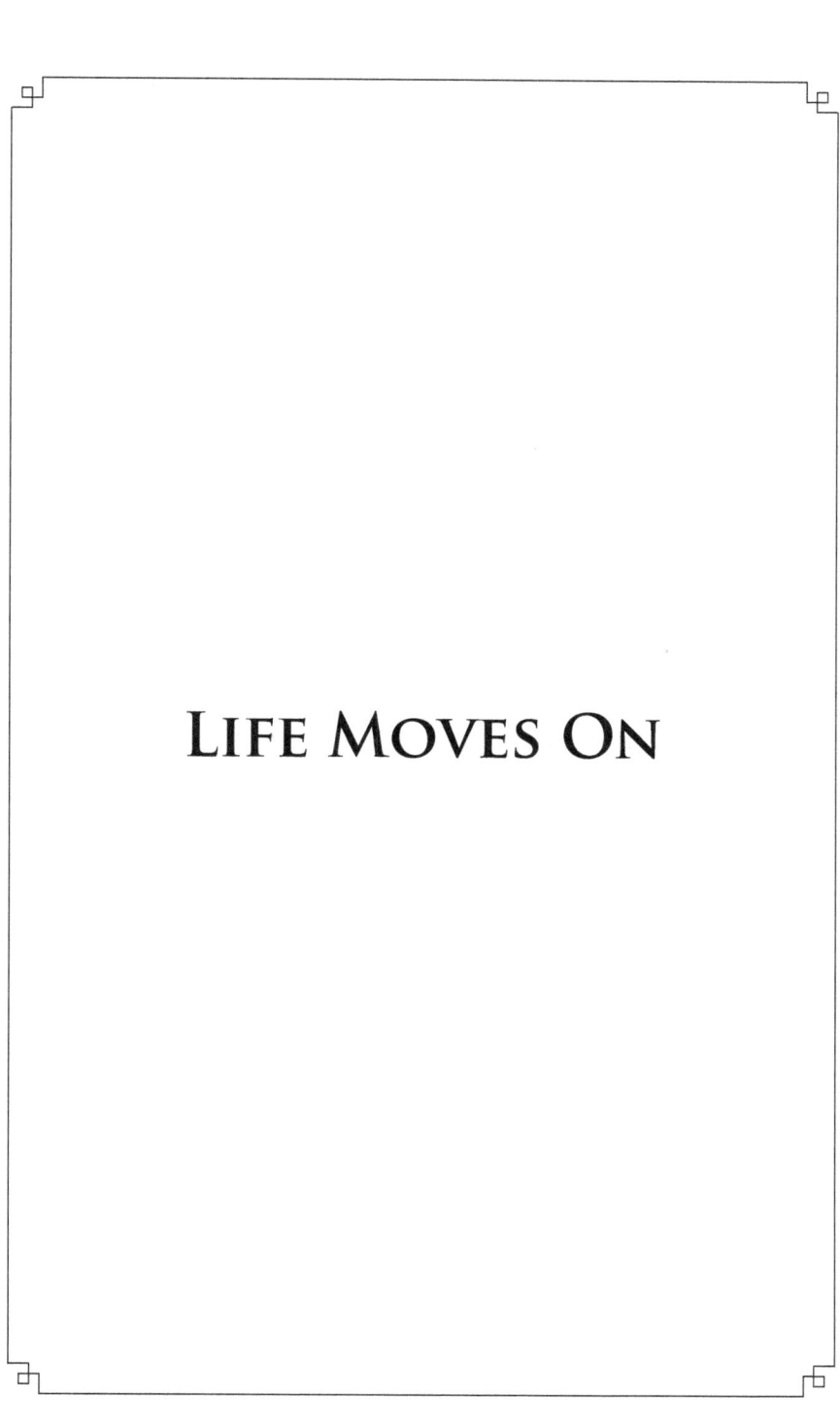

LIFE MOVES ON

As the years began to pass and as I became older, my Abuelita was right there for me every step of the way. She was there for my high school graduation in 1992, and supported me with the birth of my son. He was born in 1993 and his mother and I were not in a relationship. My ex made it extremely difficult for me to visit him, and my Abuelita jumped in and played the "Middle Man", convincing my ex to allow me to see my son. My Abuelita opened her home to my ex, allowing her to come by and drop him off.

My Abuelita also helped my wife plan my surprise 30th birthday party, and she was there for my wedding, but her health began to decline. I would visit her daily after work and during my days off during the week, but that was not enough. My *padrino* convinced her to move out of the home that I grew up in and into his old house in Clovis, Ca. She moved into his old house and lived in Clovis for several years, but eventually, as her health continued to decline, she moved into a retirement village for seniors.

Some time later, my Abuelita began to get dizzy spells and was frequently falling. She was no longer able to drive or live on her own. She then decided to live with my mother and my mother's husband, Rock, and during this time, she lost the use of both of her legs and was confined to a wheelchair. During the years my grandmother lived with my mother, I could not see her due to my mother's hatred for my wife and me.

My mother never forgave me for marrying a Black woman, and this would also be my mother's chance to enact "revenge" on my grandmother for the relationship she and I had.

For my grandmother to live with my mother and get whatever care she could receive from her, my mother made it clear to my grandmother that as long as she was living in my mother's house and receiving my mother's care, my grandmother would have no contact with me. My grandmother reluctantly complied with my mother's demands; I would not see my grandmother for over ten years.

My grandmother became tired of the neglectful treatment she received from my mother and Rock and moved into a nursing home/care facility. It was at this nursing facility where she contracted pneumonia and was rushed to the hospital, and she remained in ICU for several weeks.

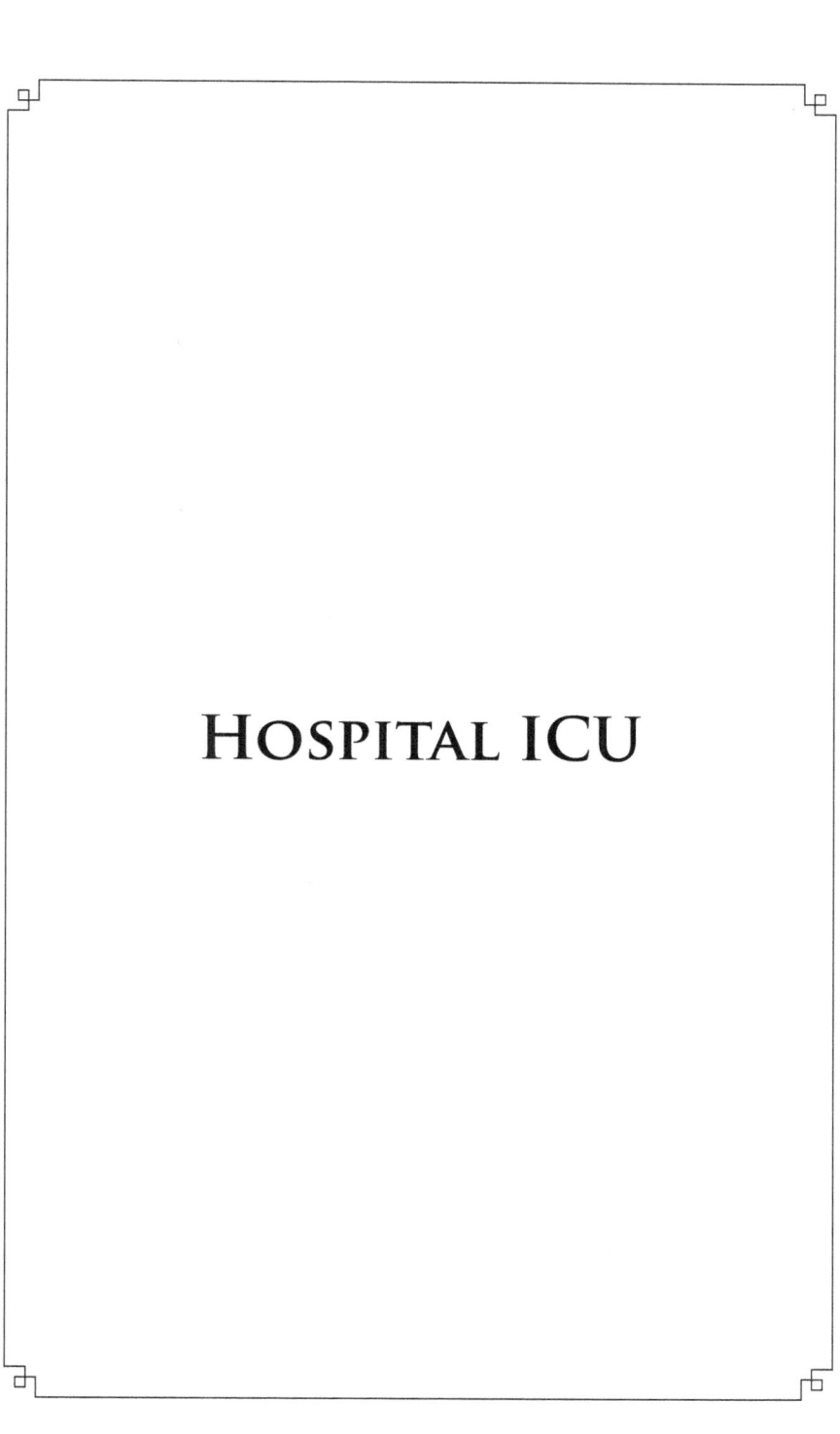

HOSPITAL ICU

Igot a phone call late one evening from one of my cousins. It was a cousin I had not spoken to or heard from for over a decade. He did not have my cell phone number, but was able to contact me via Facebook. My phone rang, so I answered, and my cousin was in tears, trying hard to keep his composure as he spoke. "Hey, cuzz, I'm sorry to tell you, I'm not sure if you've heard, but your mom is in the hospital." I casually and unsympathetically replied, "Oh wow, that's too bad." He detected the sarcasm in my voice and said, "No, cuzz, your *REAL MOM*, your Abuelita."

He explained that my Abuelita was rushed to the hospital, was admitted to the ICU, and was hooked up to a ventilator. He told me he was unsure how much more time she had, so I should go and visit her as soon as possible. I could feel the tears rolling down my face as I asked him which floor she was on and her room number. He gave me the information and informed me that seeing her that evening was impossible because visiting hours were already over. I thanked him for the information as we ended our phone call.

I fell to the floor as my knees buckled. I lay on the carpet like a baby, crying uncontrollably. My wife heard me and came rushing down the hallway. She didn't have to ask me what had happened as she entered the room. As a mother herself, she instinctively knew that the sound of my sobbing could only mean one thing... I was losing my Abuelita. My wife sat on the floor and held me while I cried. After a couple of hours, I was able to muster up enough strength to call the hospital. I gave them my Abuelitas name, asked for her room number, and asked what time they were visiting hours.

I was unable to sleep. I lay in bed and stared at the ceiling, reminiscing about all the wonderful childhood memories of my Abuelita. I had to be at work at 7 am, so I got up, got dressed, and headed to the hospital to see her before I went to work.

I arrived at the hospital at around 5:30 am. I wanted to be at the hospital, near her, as close as possible to her, hoping that she could feel my presence. I made my way off of the elevator and walked into the ICU. I asked for her room number, and one of the staff members pointed me in the right direction. I walked to her room and slowly walked in.

My Abuelita was lying in bed. She had multiple IVs in her arms and was very pale looking. She was fragile and hooked up to a ventilator and heart monitor. There was a chair in her room, so I grabbed it and moved it to the corner behind the door. I was not supposed to be in the room because visiting hours had not yet started, and I didn't want anyone to kick me out. I sat in the chair. I lowered my head... I prayed... I cried.

I'm not sure how much time had passed when I heard a woman's voice whisper, "Ohh, you startled me!" I looked up, and a female nurse entered the room. I stood up and replied, "I'm sorry; I didn't mean to scare you. I know I'm not supposed to be here; I just wanted to be with my Abuelita." The nurse smiled and said, "You're Jaime, aren't you?" I looked at her trying to figure out how she knew my name. She recognized the curious look on my face and smiled. She said, "The night Esperanza was admitted into the hospital, all she kept talking about was her 'little Jaimito'."

The tears began to flow down my cheeks. The woman smiled and softly said, "Ohhhh no, don't cry. You're going to make me cry." Her eyes began to water as she said, "You can go over to her and say hi; I think she is awake. Your Abuelita has been waking up very early these last few mornings." I wiped the tears from my eyes as I told the nurse, "Thank you."

I walked over to the side of my Abuelita's bed. Her head was turned to her left, so she did not see me walking up to her. I reached down and held her hand; it was so soft and frail. I said softly, "*Buenos días, mamá*[61]," as my tears began to flow again. My Abuelita slowly turned her head towards me and opened her eyes.

She stared at me for a while with a look of early-morning grogginess as she tried to focus on my face for a second, then she closed her eyes. I leaned over, closed my eyes, and softly

---

61 "Good morning, mother."

kissed her forehead. As I kissed her, my mind began to race, flashing back to all the wonderful childhood memories of my Abuelita and me. With each beautiful memory, my body began to tremble, and I began to cry a little bit harder.

Time seemed to stand still as I stood there. I let go of her hand, reached over her bed, and grabbed the raised guard rail. I took my left arm and placed it above her pillow to support my weight as I leaned over to put my head next to her ear. Fighting through my tears, I whispered, *"Lo siento por no venir a verte. Lo siento por permitir que el odio que le tenia a mi madre me alejara de ti. No estoy listo para perderte. Por favor, perdóname. Por favor no me dejes. Por favor, no te vayas*[62].*"*

I lay there, hugging my Abuelita, crying uncontrollably. I cried for a good couple of minutes; then, my crying turned to sniffles. I lay there holding my Abuelita as I listened to the slow rhythmic beeping of her heart monitor. Then, I noticed the beeping of her monitor slowly began to increase. I raised my head slightly and looked at the monitor, wiping away my tears. The beeping increased a little more. I looked down at my Abuelita, and she slowly looked up to see who was holding her. I stood up and took a step back so she could see me. This time, her eyes were able to focus on my face. She slowly raised her hands and covered her mouth as she was overcome with

---

62 "I'm sorry for not coming to see you. I'm sorry for allowing my hatred for my mother to keep me away from you. I'm not ready to lose you. Please forgive me. Please don't leave me. Please don't go."

so much emotion; she shouted as strongly as possible, "*¡¡Ay, MIJO!!*" and began to weep.

She looked down at my feet, then looked up at my face again and shouted, "*Oh Jaime, ay, mijito,*" and she opened her arms for a hug. I leaned down and hugged her as she began to cry uncontrollably. "*Mijito, mijito, mijito… Sabia que te volveria a ver*[63]," she cried.

"*Lo siento mucho por no verte antes…*[64]" I began to tell her. She interrupted me and said, "*Nada de eso importa. Dios contestó mis oraciones. He rezado todos los días para verte de nuevo antes de irme, y ahora estás aquí*[65]."

I didn't go to work that day. I sat at the hospital for hours with my Abuelita. We laughed, talked, and reminisced about all the trouble I got into and the danger she got me out of. I got a chance to thank her for all the unconditional love and wonderful childhood memories I have because of her; I got a chance to love and hold her one last time….

My Abuelita passed away a few months later.

---

63   "Son, son, son… I knew I would see you again."
64   "I'm so sorry for not seeing you sooner."
65   "None of that matters. God answered my prayers. I've prayed every day for years to see you again before I leave, and you are here now."

LOSING MY ABUELITA

When I lost my Abuelita, it did not hit me at first. I mean, I went to her funeral. I stood at her casket and said goodbye, but for some reason, I did not cry. I couldn't cry. How could I not? What was wrong with me? This woman was everything to me. She was a force to be reckoned with during the most crucial times of my life. She loved me the way my biological mother should have loved me, but I was not sad for some reason. I realized many years later that I didn't have any real emotion for the loss of my Abuelita because I subconsciously refused to believe she was gone. While I was sitting in the chapel, my mind would only replay all of the beautiful memories I had of her. I would not succumb to the loss of my Abuelita until almost one year later.

In 2015, I drove commercially throughout California for a company delivering books to schools. I would provide books and reading materials to elementary, junior high, and high schools. I also delivered these reading materials to elementary schools on several military bases, such as Edwards Air Force base, Lemoore Naval Air Station, and China Lake Naval Weapons Air Station. I did a lot of driving. Well over 2,500 miles a week.

One day, I was returning to Fresno. I was driving on the old highway 41 coming through Caruthers. I was approaching an old Elm Avenue gas station with a WW2 fighter plane buried nose down in the roof above the gas pumps. I got a few miles down the road when I got this odd feeling. I began to breathe heavily like I was having a panic attack, only I wasn't panicking. I looked for a place to pull over, and I pulled my truck off the road onto the dirt shoulder. I took my vehicle out of gear, applied my park brakes, put on my hazard lights, and leaned back in my seat. There was something about that gas station, something about seeing that airplane...

Then it hit me. I could feel my chest, heart, lungs, and stomach begin to fill with grief in a way that I had never felt before. The tears started flowing as I was overcome with a sadness unfamiliar to me. I covered my face with my hands and began to cry. I was so weak with grief that I couldn't sit up in my seat. I leaned over on the steering wheel, sobbing, as I called out, "Abuelita."

It had been decades since I had traveled down Elm Avenue. My Abuelita used to take me on country drives when I was a child. We would get in the car and go for a ride with no particular destination in mind. Many of these drives would take place on Sunday evenings. After spending the weekends with her, I would refuse to go home to my mother and Rock, so my Abuelita would drive around for hours and hours, talking and singing to me until I fell asleep. One of the images

I remembered as I was falling asleep was the unusual sight of that airplane, nose down on the roof.

My Abuelita was my everything. Without her during my childhood and teenage years, I don't believe I would have made it to adulthood. My Abuelita cared for me, adored me, and showered me with a love so unconditional that no earthly position could ever determine its value. I have only known of one other love like this—the unconditional love I receive from my wife.

My Abuelita gave me the best of both worlds. She raised me to be a proud Mexican and never ashamed to admit that I have Mexicano[66] blood running through my veins. She also raised me to be a proud African American and a proud Blackman, and she told me one day, I would learn to love my dark skin color just as much as she had.

I'm sure you are wondering how my Abuelita, a 4 ft. 10" old Mexican woman from Guadalajara, Mexico, with very limited English, taught me how to "be Black". She didn't. She couldn't. Like myself, she knew nothing about Black life or Black culture… so she did the next best thing she could think of: she integrated Michael Jackson into her Mariachi and Vicente Fernandez music rotation. She got me into Martial Arts and took me to get a Jeri curl because I wanted to be like Bruce Leroy from the 1985 movie *The Last Dragon*. She took a significant interest in and developed a love for hip-hop

---

66 Mexican.

and rap music and cheered me on in local breakdancing and rap battles. And although I was raised on a diet of nopales[67], tamales[68], menudo[69], homemade flour tortillas *con mantequilla*[70], *albóndigas*[71], quesadillas[72], horchata[73], and *pan dulce*[74]... She managed to make me *chorizo con huevos y papas*[75] on Sunday mornings before church, and **KFC** with biscuits and gravy Sunday evenings after church.

---

67 A type of cacti used in Mexican cuisine.
68 A traditional dish consisting in a cornmeal dough filled with meat or beans, wrapped in banana leaf or corn husk and steamed.
69 A traditional beef tripe stew.
70 With butter.
71 Meatballs.
72 A dish consisting of a flour tortilla folded in half and filled with cheese, meats and other ingredients.
73 A sweet, usually plant-based cold drink made with rice or almonds, with a cinnamon or vanilla flavour.
74 Sweet bread or buns which are often baked in the form of seashells.
75 Chorizo with fried eggs and fried potatoes.

Gracias por todo Abuelita. Te amo[76].

Thanks for everything, Abuelita. I love you.

www.ingramcontent.com/pod-product-compliance
Lightning Source LLC
Chambersburg PA
CBHW082106140626
46553CB00018B/1096